La Jolla

A Pictorial Tour

DEDICATION

FOR ELLEN BROWNING SCRIPPS WHOSE DEDICATED,
CONSTRUCTIVE PHILANTHROPIES AND UNWAVERING
SOCIAL VISION HELPED STEER THE RIGHT COURSE IN
THE GROWTH AND DEVELOPMENT OF LA JOLLA.

PHOTOGRAPHS BY

ERIC MASTERMAN

TEXT BY

MICHAEL DORMER

ARCAS PUBLICATIONS

SAN DIEGO CALIFORNIA

U S A

La Jolla

A PICTORIAL TOUR

BY
ERIC MASTERMAN

PUBLISHED AND DISTRIBUTED BY ARCAS PUBLICATIONS

PHOTOGRAPHY BY ERIC MASTERMAN

TEXT BY MICHAEL DORMER

COVER DESIGN BY GRAPHIC DETAILS

BOOK DESIGN BY GRAPHIC DETAILS

LA JOLLA MAP REPRODUCED BY PERMISSION.
LA JOLLA BLUE BOOK PUBLISHERS, INC.

FIRST EDITION, FIRST PRINTING — 2003

ISBN 0-9615753-4-4

ARCAS PUBLICATIONS
1666 Garnet Avenue, PMB 505, San Diego, California 92109
www.arcaspublications.com

PRINTED IN THE UNITED STATES OF AMERICA.

CONTENTS

INTRODUCTION

On February 27, 1869, Samuel Sizer and his brother Daniel purchased two lots on some coastal 'pueblo lands' north of San Diego for $1.25 an acre. They planted grapevines on the barren turf south of 'La Joya' valley but they weren't really the first settlers in the area. Indian communities predated the Sizers by thousands of years and stone metates for grinding corn and other utensils, relics, and burial mounds, are still routinely being discovered.

In the hundred and thirty plus years since Sam and Dan tended their grapes, La Jolla has gone through many cultural and physical changes but has never lost its inherent charm. Today human scale luxury hotels and fine restaurants abound and walkabouts reveal countless quaint boutiques brimming with fascinating items. Stately cliffs and beautiful beaches front the rugged coastline and there's an abundant supply of flora and fauna here to tickle the fancies of the most ardent naturalists. A great university sits on top of the mesa north of town, while barely a mile away is a world famous oceanographic institution.

A long time hangout for artists and writers, musicians and movie stars, movers and shakers, and con men and kings, it's no wonder they call this town with its multifaceted personality, 'The Jewel.'

'La Joya,' pronounced 'la-HOY-yah,' means 'The Jewel' in Spanish. Somehow in the town's early history, two 'l's' replaced the 'y,' so the spelling was changed to 'La JoLLa' but the old pronunciation was retained. In any case, 'La Jolla' as 'The Jewel' describes the place perfectly and it's a bit more elegant than the ancient slightly similar Native American name that loosely translates into 'the place full of holes,' which probably had something to do with the town's many caves in its seaside cliffs.

LA JOLLA MAP

1- Whispering Sands

2- Bird Rock

3- Windansea Beach

4- The Children's Pool

5- The Cove

6- Ellen Browning Scripps Park

7- The Cave Store

8- Coast Walk

9- Girard Avenue

10- Prospect Street

11- Museum of Contemporary Art

12- Saint James By-The-Sea

13- John Cole's Book Shop

14- La Jolla Shores Beach

15- La Jolla Beach & Tennis Club

16- Scripps Institution of Oceanography

17- Birch Aquarium-Museum

18- University of California, SD

19- The Mormon Temple

20- Torrey Pines Cliffs

21- Torrey Pines Gliderport

22- Torrey Pines Golf Course

23- Torrey Pines State Reserve

24- Mount Soledad

*Just match up the numbers of the places listed that you might wish to visit
with the corresponding numbers on the map and you're on your way.*

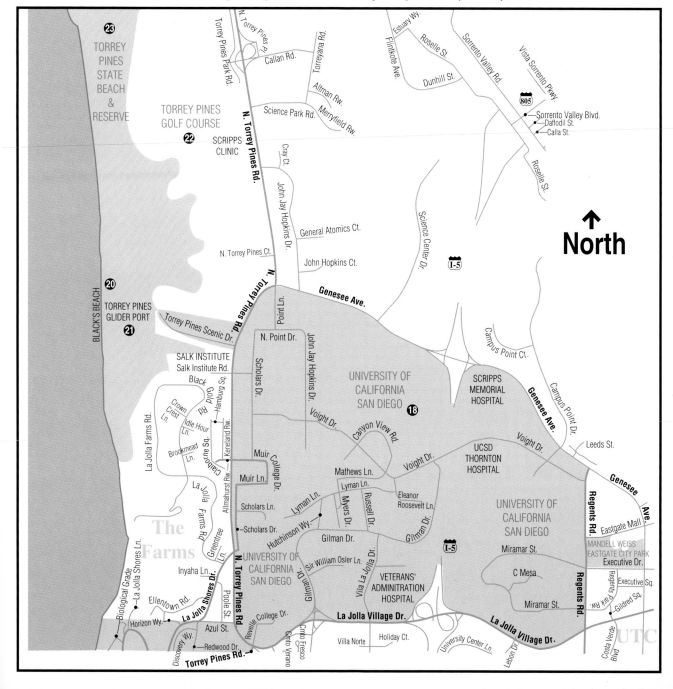

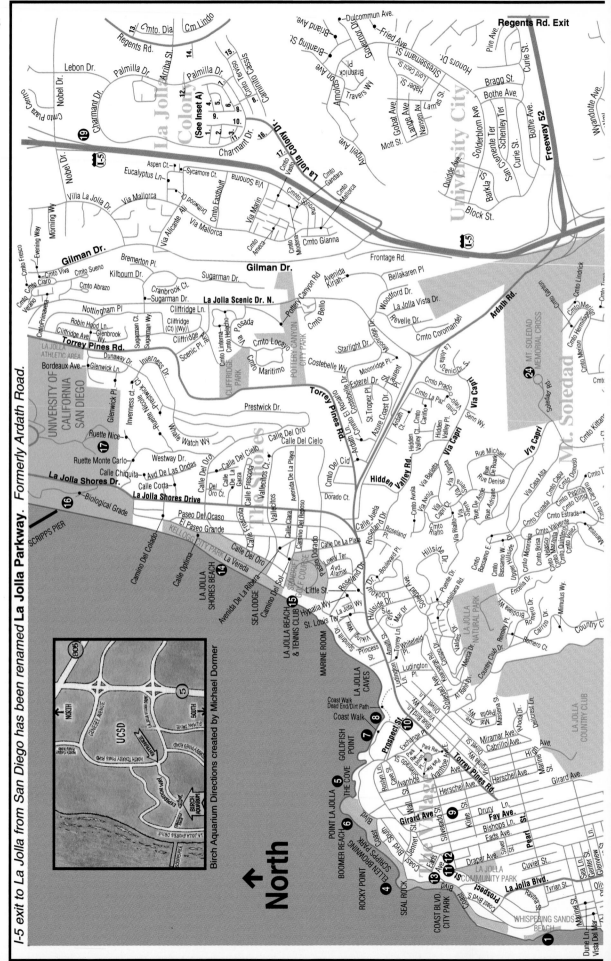

North

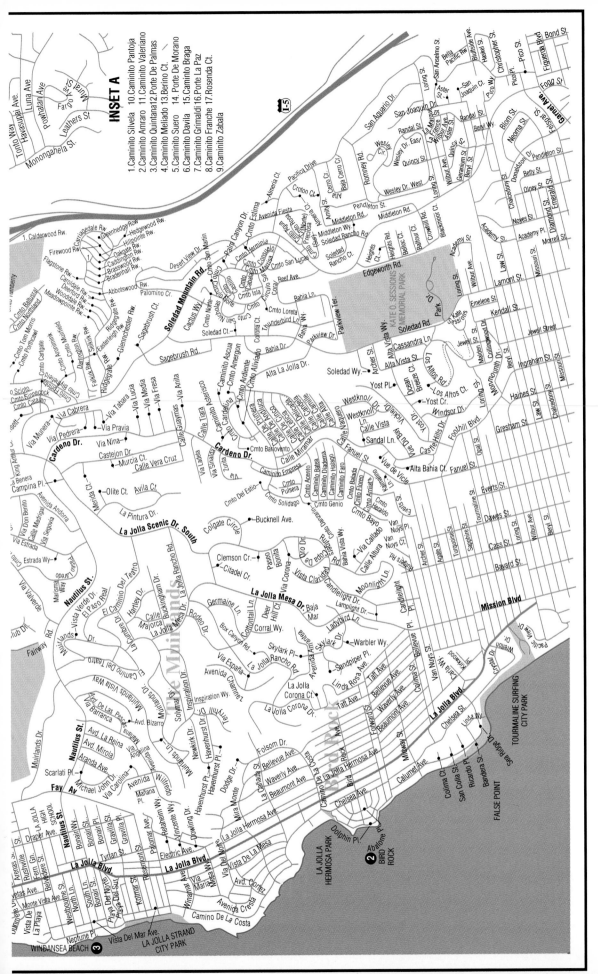

THE VILLAGE

La Jolla's first recorded land owner, unlucky Sam Sizer, fell down a well in 1870 putting an abrupt end to both himself and his struggling vineyard. What became of his bereaved brother is a history mystery. The development of La Jolla languished until 1886 when Frank T. Botsford snapped up four hundred acres, of what was then known as 'La Jolla Park,' for $2200. He and some partners chopped the property up into saleable lots, the choicest ones going for the then lofty price of $3000. Thus began the area's land boom.

As the years rolled by, accessibility through improvements in transportation brought people to La Jolla in droves and many of them stayed and the town grew. Uncontrolled growth can sometimes pollute pretty places, but a tour of 'The Jewel' today clarifies the efforts of early civic leaders who exercised enough intelligent urban planning and control with uncommon foresight that kept the town from becoming an unattractive hodgepodge. Picture La Jolla today as a grand gourmet meal: a generous serving of prime California, flavored with just a tasty dash of European spice.

LA JOLLA SHORES

Cattle used to roam this long wide beach during the day, while opium smugglers landed their illicit cargoes in the dark of night nearly a century ago.

Things have been slicked up some since those simpler times and La Jolla Shores has morphed into a pleasant model of upscale seaside suburban living full of informal, friendly folks in shorts and flip flops. It's best described as Southern California style at its best.

WHISPERING SANDS

The unique 'sand that speaks' on the beach and in the little coves just north of Windansea Beach makes strange whispering sounds with every step you take.

BIRD ROCK

There's a pretty little spot a mile or so south of La Jolla's village where the sun always shines its best. Descriptively named after a huge stone in the ocean with seabirds always perched on top, Bird Rock was once the mother lode for hungry divers who greedily over-fished the tasty and plentiful abalone in the waters there until the jumbo-sized mollusks, with their gleaming mother-of-pearl inner shells, became nearly extinct. There's even a street named 'Abalone Place' which, of course, no longer really applies in this low-key, fun to visit suburb with its pleasant shops, restaurants and hotels.

WINDANSEA BEACH

Ground Zero for the planet's most skillful board surfers for decades, this picture-perfect beach is a veritable gold-mine for photographers. The palm frond covered 'shack,' a designated historical site, dates back to the '30s and was, and still is, the gathering place of some of the most wildly colorful and eccentric characters ever to 'hang ten' in the slamming shorebreak. It's a good place to pick up a tan or for just ambling about, but not a swimmer's treat due to riptides, rough water, and other hazards. If you're still determined to give it a go, better wear your water wings. A cubical concrete city utility building hugs the cliff just south of the shack. A Tom Wolfe novel spotlighted a high spirited, offbeat beach bunch that used to hang out there, 'The Pumphouse Gang,' and made them into curious literary stars.

(Above) The great waves at Windansea were created solely for surfing according to this high-spirited young athlete. (Below) ...And then there are the gentler and less driven souls who believe that the restless waters exist purely for the purpose of peaceful contemplation.

THE CHILDREN'S POOL

Ellen Browning Scripps, a much loved and respected community activist, decided that the little children of La Jolla needed a safe place to swim so she commissioned a breakwater to be built to shelter a small cove in front of what is now known as 'The Casa de Mañana' retirement home. The children's pool was completed in 1931 and the kids flocked to it in droves. As time went on, pleasure seeking seals were attracted to the calm, rippling waters and warm, comfy sands and eventually took over the aqua corral, reducing the little tykes to second class surf citizens. The odd pecking order continues to this day due to the stalwart efforts of animal rights activists citing the 'Marine Mammal Protection Act' which infers that banishment of the seals goes against the higher laws of Mother Nature. A hot pro and con seal debate rages on as of this writing.

The jury on the breakwater at the Children's Pool ponders the seals' impassioned pleas for sovereignty. The foreman suggests throwing 'em a fish.

THE COVE

The cove is the jewel in the crown of the 'Ellen B. Scripps Memorial Park.' Early visitors to this toy-like beach noted that its western cliff formations looked a lot like a huge alligator with a cave-punctured promontory resembling the beast's head. Someone christened the point 'Alligator Head,' and the name stuck. Weathering, wave action, and time eventually caused the roof of the cave to collapse, so today the cove's popular stone saurian more closely resembles a giant reclining Rottweiler. The cove offers beach folk coarse, comfortable, crunchy sand, gentle swimmable surf, and topnotch snorkeling. Tank and free divers might as well leave their abalone irons and lobster bags at home though, because the cove, once known as a fresh seafood cornucopia, is now a protected fish and game preserve. The annual 'Rough Water Swim' is also a star attraction.

ELLEN BROWNING SCRIPPS PARK

After intensive shopping and a lunch in the village, it's probably time for an R&R break from the traffic and the lively crowd. Just a short stroll down the hill from the western dead-end of Girard Avenue, and perched on top of the cliffs above the sea, lies the Ellen B. Scripps Memorial Park, La Jolla's tribute to the lady who gave so much. This handily located getaway zone, with its majestic palms, lush lawns, colorful flower gardens, meandering cliffside paths, and fresh sea breezes, is guaranteed to drain the stress out of even the most hard core, type 'A' personalities. A sooth-

ing, surf-accented sunset at the park can be spectacular at times, and remember to watch for the rare and elusive 'green flash' as the sun does its final dip on the horizon.

Relaxed visitors lazily walk off their kinks on a meandering park path while old-time wind-shaped trees dream of days of La Jolla long past.

THE CAVE STORE

This charming establishment has been in continuous operation since 1902, when its founder, Dr. Gustav Schulz, rolled into town and purchased the property that included the famous 'Sunny Jim' cave — then only accessible from the ocean. Schulz had a long tunnel dug down to the cave from his newly opened curio shop and, for a small fee, he hosted educational geology tours for amateur spelunkers in the spooky grotto. The quirky professor was often spotted during his off hours floating on his back in nearby waters smoking a pipe and wearing a hat. Surprisingly, he developed a bit of a 'Don Juan' reputation with the local ladies who were shocked to learn after his death that the cad had been secretly married for years and had coldly deserted a wife and a brood of children in Wisconsin.

The sale of illegal whiskey during prohibition and dollars garnered from smuggling aliens added some shady, under-the-table income to the revenue from the curios and cave tours in darker bygone days. The more legitimate business practice of renting the facility for pirate movie location shots has also helped make The Cave Store a consistent money maker for more than one hundred years.

SUNNY JIM CAVE

Frank Baum, author of the unforgettable children's books about the wonderful "Land of Oz," purportedly named this cave 'Sunny Jim' because he thought the opening resembled the profile of a pirate's head. It's the only cave in the cliffs that is accessible by land.

COAST WALK

A mellow La Jolla day. A colorful flower-bordered path. A million-dollar view of the cliffs and the shores. 'Vegging out' on a comfortable bench. It's as close as one can get to sheer contentment.

(Above) *The mysterious 'Seven Sisters' cave area.*   (Below) *The pelican club holds its daily meeting.*

You're headed off to the hub of the town, so lace up your tennies and get ready for a walk on the wild side. Girard Avenue and Prospect Street are 'action central' for high-energy shopping, sumptuous dining, and exciting nightlife. On the other hand, if you're in a laid-back mood, you can simply park yourself on a comfortable bench and spend your time people-watching the seemingly endless passing parade of colorful locals and tourists.

MUSEUM OF CONTEMPORARY ART

Ellen Scripps hired noted local architect Irving Gill to design and construct a new fire-proof home on Prospect Street to replace her previous one, 'South Moulton Villa,' which had been recently torched by a deranged drunken arsonist. It was Miss Scripps' wish that after her death the new home would be utilized as a community service building. Strikingly modern in concept even by today's standards, the handsome concrete and stucco structure went through several modifications and name changes before becoming the 'Museum of Contemporary Art'. It's come a long way since Ellen's informal garden tours and stimulating art soirees enlivened the place from the late teens to the early thirties and the facility today, which features only outstanding examples of modern art conceived after 1950, is considered by connoisseurs to be one of the leading contemporary museums in the world.

Even if you're not nuts about modern art and don't know the difference between a Picasso and a pistachio, a tour of the impressive premises is still well worth the price of admission. The soul-satisfying coastal views from the expansive picture windows, plus the beautiful sculpture garden make this Museum one of La Jolla's highlights.

Rare vintage dwellings and other tasty La Jolla sightings captured by blinks of the all-seeing camera eye.

SAINT JAMES BY-THE-SEA

This attractive Episcopal church is located across the street near the art museum and is just one of many places of worship in town.

JOHN COLE'S BOOK SHOP

'The Wisteria Cottage' was built in 1904, by Ellen Scripps, for her free-spirited half sister Virginia and still stands today as a well-preserved example of turn of the century Craftsman style architecture.

Imbued with the traditional Scripps bent for philanthropy and obsessive in her penchant for neatness, sister Virginia helped fund the Bishop's School with the proviso that trees would be banned from the campus because they would just dirty up the place. She was often seen vigorously sweeping up trash around the town armed with her trusty broom and wheelbarrow. A street in La Jolla, 'Virginia Way,' is named after the energetic and flamboyant lady.

Ellen Scripps had a passion for the written word and would have undoubtedly been delighted that Virginia's bungalow, with its signature wisteria-covered pergola, would endure and be reinvented as a picturesque and well-stocked book shop.

LA JOLLA SHORES BEACH

It's La Jolla's big beach with plenty of room for surfers, joggers, swimmers, and sun-seeking beach potatoes. Volleyball champs sharpen up their 'spikes' here and the inshore waters are generally benign enough for the wee ones to splash around in. The imposing Scripps pier, a pure research facility and off-limits to the public, traces a line to the Scripps Institution of Oceanography building complex nestled in the bluffs at the north end of the beach. The little village, just a short walk back from the south end, features inviting bistros if 'the need to feed' hits you. A quiet early morning stroll on the shores beach can be your personal journey to nirvana.

(Above) Maybe the tumultuous surf at Windansea has proven too challenging this day, so some intrepid water-men prepare to ride their boards on the kinder, gentler waves of 'The Shores.'

(Below) Today's little splashers just might wind up tomorrow's big surfers.

LA JOLLA BEACH AND TENNIS CLUB

The La Jolla Beach and Tennis Club bumps up against the shores village. It's a luxurious private facility, but it's unique 'Marine Room' restaurant is open to the public. Get set for a memorable treat if you chance to dine there during an extra-high tide when the playful surf just might start caressing the large, hurricane-proof picture windows.

SCRIPPS INSTITUTION OF OCEANOGRAPHY

In 1905, a building nicknamed 'The Little Green Laboratory' was constructed at La Jolla Cove just above 'Alligator Head' rock. It was the headquarters of the newly formed 'Marine Biological Association of San Diego,' and was the brainchild of Dr. William E. Ritter who was head of the biology department at the University of California. Soon more room was needed for bigger aquariums and more research equipment so, as always, the beneficent Scripps clan jumped in with financing for a new facility located at the north end of La Jolla Shores. In one of the truly great land deals of all time, one hundred and seventy acres of prime, ocean front property was sold on the public auction block to Ritter's institute for $1000. The name was soon changed to 'The Scripps Institution of Oceanography,' but early wisecracking locals tagged it 'The Bug House.' Since its humble beginnings, the institute has gone on to become an international giant in oceanographic research, attracting the world's leading scientists and experts in that fascinating field and architecturally it's a far cry from the shack-like 'green lab' of the cove days. Today, modern, environmentally friendly structures mesh pleasantly with old-time, well-preserved research bungalows, and the handsome, state-of-the-art suspension bridge that spans La Jolla Shores Drive near the institute is a definite 'must see.'

THE BIRCH AQUARIUM

Detailed map directions on page 6

The creaky old 1950's era aquarium at Scripps had become cramped for exhibit space, so the powers-that-be decided that it was time for a new one. A spectacular hilltop location was chosen and construction began. In September of 1992, the generously endowed, 31,000 square foot, 'Birch Aquarium' was opened to the public. Fourteen million well-spent dollars have produced an extraordinary ocean view complex that rivals any other aquarium anywhere, and you'll feel like you're swimming with the fishes as you gaze into the numerous tanks brimming with improbable sea creatures happily at home in their re-created habitats. The 'Birch' also features a realistic outdoor tide pool, fascinating ocean related exhibits, and an eye-popping giant kelp forest complete with menacing sharks and other big and little fish that normally lurk around those interesting plants in the wild. Whale watching, interesting lectures, and a wide variety of other activities can be ordered up on the aquarium-museum's extensive menu. And, speaking of menus, snacks are available outdoors near the entrance if you crave a little nourishment.

(Top left) Is it an animal or a vegetable? The incredible 'Leafy Sea Dragon' keeps you guessing.

(Top right) Looks like something fishy is going on in the giant kelp forest.

(Above) Overheard: 'It's a darn good thing this isn't a petting zoo.'

(Lower right) They're as beautiful and fragile as flowers but the sting from a brush with the wrong jellyfish can be horrendous.

UNIVERSITY OF CALIFORNIA AT SAN DIEGO

Dr. Roger Revelle's dream became reality in May of 1959 when the Regents of the University of California okayed his plan to establish a major university in the La Jolla area. A similar concept had been fielded in the 1920's but had come to a dead end. Revelle's and colleague Carl Eckart's intelligent and thoughtfully conceived proposal achieved crystallization in 1962, when the University of California, San Diego, first opened its doors. UCSD has since matured into an internationally lauded model for excellence in science, medical research and education, as well as the arts and humanities and a myriad of other fields of study. In short, UCSD does it all and does it extremely well. The Scripps Institution of Oceanography is also a part of the university. A walking tour around this gorgeous campus with its cutting-edge architecture and tasteful landscaping just might inspire you to go back to school and pick up another degree or two.

(Below) The Humanities and Social Sciences complex features well-equipped 'kitchens' cooking up innovative new recipes for meaningful social progress.

(Above) Named in honor of Theodor (Dr. Seuss) Geisel and his wife, Audrey, the stunning Geisel library glorifies the skyline of this futuristic city of learning.

(Below) The Revelle College of Physics is the ultimate 'smart farm' where students and researchers relentlessly delve into what makes our mysterious universe tick.

THE MORMON TEMPLE

With its two main spires jutting skyward, one topped by a golden angel blowing a horn, the Mormon Temple architecturally echos a fanciful fairytale castle mercifully omitting the usual frilly details, and the light play on its carefully scaled flat surfaces emphasizes the basic purity of its balanced design. It's a spiritually visual treat and a blessed relief from the all too numerous, lookalike, corporate style buildings that seem to dominate today's urban landscapes. The temple is located inland from the village and is visible from highway 5. It is not open to the public.

TORREY PINES CLIFFS

They're not as big as 'Big Sur,' but they convey their own distinct and unparalleled majesty. Look out over the sea from those towering cliffs and you'll feel like the king or queen of the world.

TORREY PINES GLIDERPORT

Local surfer and gliding ace Woody Brown flew the first glider off the Torrey pines cliffs way back in 1935. Since then, thousands of airborne daredevils have ridden the wild thermals near the gliderport in an incredible variety of motorless flying machines.

TORREY PINES GOLF COURSE

Duffers and pros alike savor this challenging championship course overlooking the sea with gusto. The popular greens are always full, so its best to book your turn well in advance. The clubhouse is a relaxing place to sip post-links cocktails, tell tall 'hole in one' tales, and compare miracle putters.

TORREY PINES STATE PRESERVE

The gnarled and scrubby 'Soledad Pines' grew mostly in one particular spot on the California coast north of La Jolla and European sailors used the forest as a chart point during early explorations. Botanist Charles Christopher Parry scrambled up the forbidding three hundred foot cliffs in 1850 and 'officially discovered' and renamed the rare conifers 'Pinus Torreyana,' or 'Torrey Pines.' 'The Torrey Pines Free and Public Park' was established in 1899 to safeguard the trees and the surrounding fragile ecosystem. Today the park boasts about two thousand acres of protected land featuring miles of inviting hiking trails plus a large, rare salt marsh in the Sorrento Valley south of the railroad tracks where bird watchers can ogle exotic waterfowl. A rustic adobe brick lodge, financed by Ellen Scripps and built in 1923, blends in beautifully with the wild and unspoiled scenery.

MOUNT SOLEDAD

Early morning Easter services have been held on top of La Jolla's premier lookout point since 1922. The first two crosses erected on the mountain were destroyed by high winds and extreme weathering, but the latest forty-three-foot tall reinforced concrete edition, installed in 1954, seems to have beaten the jinx and is holding up well. It stands as a memorial to servicemen and women who perished in the two great world wars and other more recent conflicts. The latest additions to the site are six concentric walls inlaid with black granite plaques engraved with information about veterans, and their photos are also on display. Nearby stands a newly installed flagpole where 'Old Glory' flies proudly every day.

The three hundred and sixty degree panoramic view from the top of Mount Soledad is incomparable and it surely stirred the soul of Charles Lindbergh, 'The Lone Eagle,' when he climbed into a glider on the summit and rode the winds all the way to Del Mar one breezy afternoon on February 24th, 1927.

A quiet ceremony on top of the mountain honors those who gave so much in the service of their country.

ROBERT L. VANDEMAN
Construction Electrician G-1
U.S. Navy - Seabee
Korea

Thanks to God
This soldier to spare
His many gifts
Blessings to share
A valiant father
Who taught us to share

JOE DAVID FALLS
BT2 - E5
U.S. Navy
Vietnam

USS Bauer DE 1025
Sailor, Husband, Father and
Grandfather, a loved man.
Always and Forever,
Your Family

General
U.S. Marine Co
Commander Fleet Marine
World War I

Tarawa, Saipan, Iwo Jima,
Philippines, Haiti, France
He loved his country, his family
and his Marines.
With Appreciation

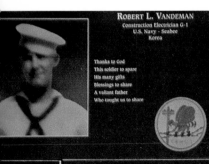

K. BARTA
lonel
Surgical Unit
ledical Corps
, D-Day - ETO
Var II

Orville E. Peterson
Captain
Fourth Infantry Division, Field Artillery
Bronze Star, Purple Heart
ETO, 5 stars and Invasion Arrowhead
World War II

D-Day, Normandy, Liberation of Paris,
No. France, Ardennes, Hurtgen Forest,
Battle of the Bulge, Rhineland,
West Germany, Liberation of Dachau.
Thank you for your sacrifice.
Our family hero. We love you always!

RAIMUND W. CHIVERS
Lieutenant

U.S. Navy
Vietnam

We Honor and cherish your
memory.

With love and pride,
Your family.

CHARLES F. DEMMLER

Captain
U.S. Navy
World War II
Korea, Vietnam

ROBERT E. KRONEMYER

Commander (Ret.)
Gunnery Officer
Naval Intelligence Officer
U.S. Naval Reserve
World War II

North Atlantic &
South Pacific Theaters

ELMER "JOE" WILSON
U.S. Army
World War II

410 U.S. Army Air Force

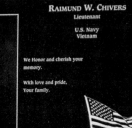

WARD F. MOO
Captain
U.S. Army
European Theate
World War II

In Loving Memory of Our Beloved

La Jolla is a very special place. No matter how much it may change on the surface, the good stuff is always there. It is in its bones.

Visitor Information:

La Jolla Visitor Center
7966 Herschel Avenue
(Herschel & Prospect)
Phone: 619-236-1212 Fax: 619-230-7084
E-mail: sdinfo@sandiego.org

Winter Hours: (Mid-Sept through Mid-June)
Thursday - Tuesday, 10:00am - 5:00pm

Summer Hours: (Mid-June through Mid-Sept)
10:00am - 7:00pm Hours subject to change.

Professional, multi-lingual, highly trained staff and volunteers will help you get the most from your visit to the San Diego region. A complete collection of current information on a wide variety of activities, attractions and dining and lodging options. Here you will be able to get a copy of The La Jolla Dining & Shopping guide, brochures, maps, a San Diego Pocket Guide, a GOLF GUIDE or a FREE Vacation Planning kit, which offers hundreds of dollars worth of savings on your trip. Everything you'll need to make your stay a memorable one!

Reference:

Readers who are interested in the history of La Jolla will find the following sources most useful.

Schaelchlin, Francis. *La Jolla – The Story of a Community.* La Jolla, CA: Friends of The La Jolla Library, 1999

Lipe, Patricia Daly & Dawson, Barbara. *La Jolla – A Celebration of It's Past.* San Diego, CA: Sunbelt Publications, 2002